THE MOHAWK

BY JOHN O'MARA

Enslow PUBLISHING

Please visit our website, www.enslow.com. For a free color catalog of all our high-quality books, call toll free 1-800-398-2504 or fax 1-877-980-4454.

Library of Congress Cataloging-in-Publication Data
Names: O'Mara, John, author.
Title: The Mohawk / John O'Mara.
Description: New York : Enslow Publishing, [2022] | Series: Native American peoples | Includes index.
Identifiers: LCCN 2020033482 (print) | LCCN 2020033483 (ebook) | ISBN 9781978521926 (library binding) | ISBN 9781978521902 (paperback) | ISBN 9781978521919 (set) | ISBN 9781978521933 (ebook)
Subjects: LCSH: Mohawk Indians–Juvenile literature. | Mohawk Indians–History–Juvenile literature.
Classification: LCC E99.M8 O44 2022 (print) | LCC E99.M8 (ebook) | DDC 974.7004/975542–dc23
LC record available at https://lccn.loc.gov/2020033482
LC ebook record available at https://lccn.loc.gov/2020033483

Published in 2022 by
Enslow Publishing
29 E. 21st Street
New York, NY 10010

Designer: Katelyn E. Reynolds
Interior Layout: Tanya Dellaccio
Editor: Therese Shea

Photo credits: Cover, p. 1 (texture) aopsan/Shutterstock.com; cvr, pp. 1–24 (striped texture) Eky Studio/Shutterstock.com; p. 4 Orchidpoet/E+/Getty Images; p. 5 SAUL LOEB/AFP/Getty Images; p. 6 Universal History Archive/Getty Images; p. 7 Interim Archives/Archive Photos/Getty Images; p. 9 (top right) Stock Montage/Archive Photos/Getty Images; p. 9 (top left) Print Collector/Hulton Archive/Getty Images; p. 9 (bottom left) Wolfgang Kaehler/LightRocket/Getty Images; pp. 10, 24, 25 (right) Bettmann/Getty Images; p. 11 4x4foto/iStock/Getty Images Plus/Getty Images; p. 13 (left) Education Images/Universal Images Group/Getty Images; p. 13 (right) FPG/Archive Photos/Getty Images; p. 14 ErikaMitchell/iStockEditorial/Getty Images Plus/Getty Images; pp. 17 (top left), 20 MPI/Archive Photos/Getty Images; p. 17 (bottom left) PHAS/Universal Images Group/Getty Images; p. 17 (bottom right) Don Dutton/Toronto Star/etty Images; p. 19 (top) https://upload.wikimedia.org/wikipedia/commons/1/10/Covenant_Chain_Wampum.jpg; p. 19 (bottom) Library of Congress/Corbis Historical/Getty Images; p. 21 (left) Stock Montage/Archive Photos/Getty Images; p. 21 (right) Interim Archives/Archive Photos/Getty Images; p. 22 Hulton Archive/Getty Images; p. 23 Fotosearch/Archive Photos/Getty Images; p. 25 (left) Bardocz Peter/Shutterstock.com; p. 27 (top left and bottom right) National Film Board of Canada/Archive Photos/Getty Images; p. 27 (top right) Alexander Spatari/Moment/Getty Images; p. 28 Christopher Morris - Corbis/Corbis Historical/Getty Images; p. 29 LARS HAGBERG/AFP/Getty Images.

Portions of this work were originally authored by Ryan Nagelhout and published as *The Mohawk People*. All new material this edition authored by John O'Mara.

CPSIA compliance information: Batch #CSENS22: For further information contact Enslow Publishing, New York, New York, at 1-800-398-2504.

Find us on

CONTENTS

WORDS IN THE GLOSSARY APPEAR IN **BOLD** TYPE THE FIRST TIME THEY ARE USED IN THE TEXT.

KEEPERS OF THE EASTERN DOOR

The Mohawk were part of the Native American group called the Haudenosaunee (hoh-DEE-noh-SHOH-nee) **Confederacy**. The Mohawk were the "keepers of the eastern door" because they were the people farthest east in this group. Their homelands were located from today's northeastern New York to southern Canada and Vermont.

FLINT

GET THE FACTS!

Where did the Mohawk come from? All Native Americans are **descended** from peoples who likely came from eastern Asia more than 12,000 years ago. These people walked over land that's now covered by the body of water called the Bering Strait.

THE NAME "MOHAWK" CAME FROM BRITISH PEOPLE. THEY GOT THE WORD FROM A NATIVE AMERICAN WORD THAT MEANS "MAN EATERS."

KANIEN'KEHÁ:KA
PEOPLE OF THE FLINT

They didn't call themselves Mohawk. Instead, they called themselves *Kanien'kehá:ka* (gah-nyuh-geh-HAW-gah), which means "people of the flint." Flint is a kind of hard rock. These people used flint they found in the earth around them to make arrow tips and other tools.

5

THE BEGINNING OF A BOND

According to native histories, a Huron man named the Peacemaker (or Dekanawidah) encouraged an Onondaga chief named Hiawatha to form a confederacy among five native peoples. These were the Mohawk, Onondaga, Oneida, Cayuga, and Seneca. This was the Haudenosaunee Confederacy. It was meant to help these nations fight against enemies and keep the peace.

HIAWATHA

THE TUSCARORA JOINED THE HAUDENOSAUNEE CONFEDERACY IN 1722. THEY HAD LIVED IN NORTH CAROLINA, BUT MOVED NORTH BECAUSE THEY HAD BEEN TREATED BADLY BY THE BRITISH.

GET THE FACTS!

The Haudenosaunee Confederacy was also called the Iroquois Confederacy or the Iroquois League. The members speak languages of the Iroquoian family of languages. British people called the group the Five Nations, and then the Six Nations once the Tuscarora joined.

MOHAWK TERRITORY

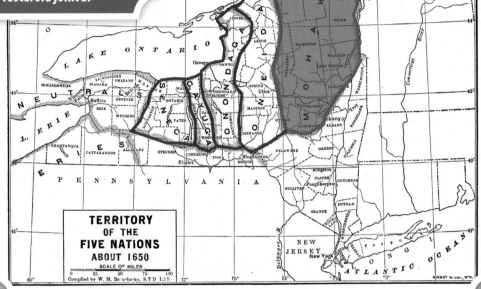

TERRITORY
OF THE
FIVE NATIONS
ABOUT 1650
SCALE OF MILES
0   25   50   75   100
Compiled by W. M. Beauchamp, S.T.D 1849.

The Mohawk were the first to accept the Peacemaker's "Great Law of Peace," a kind of **constitution**. The other groups soon followed. Each people had one vote in decisions. In 1722, the Tuscarora people joined the group.

IN THE LONGHOUSE

The Mohawk lived in homes called longhouses. In fact, all the peoples of the Haudenosaunee Confederacy did. *Haudenosaunee* means "they made the house." A longhouse is a home built from wood and bark for several families.

Longhouses were from 40 to 400 feet (12 to 122 m) long and were usually 22 or 23 feet (6.7 or 7 m) wide. Each longhouse was home to families that belonged to the same clan, or a group of families related to one another. It's believed that each family had their own section of the longhouse to live in.

HAUDENOSAUNEE: "THEY MADE THE HOUSE"

SINCE THE NATIVE AMERICANS HAD NO NAILS TO CONNECT PIECES OF THEIR LONGHOUSE, THEY TIED THEM WITH STRIPS OR ROPES OF BARK.

GET THE FACTS!

A long walkway connected one end of the longhouse to the other. A hole in the roof served as a chimney so that fires for cooking could be built inside the longhouse. In some places, longhouses had separate doors for men and women.

MOHAWK LIFE

Mohawk family life was based on the matrilineal clan. This is a word that means all female children belong to the mother's clan. After marriage, a man moved into the longhouse of his wife's clan. All females would live in the same longhouse with their mothers and their grandmothers for their entire lives.

THIS DRAWING SHOWS THE HARD WORK OF EVERYDAY LIFE IN A MOHAWK COMMUNITY.

THREE SISTERS

BEANS

SQUASH

CORN

THE "THREE SISTERS" WERE A NICKNAME FOR THE THREE MAIN CROPS OF MANY NORTH AMERICAN NATIVE PEOPLES: BEANS, SQUASH, AND CORN.

GET THE FACTS!

Mohawk women were the farmers. They grew corn, beans, peas, squash, melons, and other crops. They made soups, stews, and cornbread with them. They also grew apple trees and picked berries. They collected a sugary liquid called syrup from maple trees too.

Women also owned the family's land and decided what would grow on it. Men hunted, fished, and traded with other native peoples. They were also warriors. They had to be ready to guard their land and families.

MOHAWK DRESS

At first, Mohawk used **natural resources** around them to make their clothing. For most, this was deerskin. Both men and women wore leggings. Women often wore a long dress over them. Sometimes they wore a skirt as well. Men wore **breechcloths** over their leggings. Furs were worn in cold months. Cloth began to replace deerskin clothing when trade with Europeans began. However, the Mohawk **decorated** the cloth with beads and ribbons.

They also decorated their deerskin shoes, called moccasins. During special **ceremonies**, men wore feather caps called headdresses.

SOME OF THE OLD WAYS OF THE MOHAWK ARE STILL PASSED DOWN TO YOUNGER GENERATIONS.

GET THE FACTS!

In times of war, Mohawk men shaved their heads except for a "scalplock" down the center of their head. This look is known today as a Mohawk. Women only cut their hair after someone they loved died, to show their sadness.

THE MOHAWK LANGUAGE

The Mohawk language was only spoken, not written, for many years. In the 1700s, French priests came to North America to teach the Mohawk about Christianity. The priests used 12 letters of the alphabet for the Mohawk language: a e h i k n o r s t w y. They also used these marks: ' and :

In the Mohawk language, *she:kon* (shay-kohn) is a friendly way to say hello. *Nia:wen* (nee-ah-wehn) means "thank you." Sometimes, just one word in Mohawk can mean a whole sentence in English!

WELCOME TO AKWESASNE
"SEKON"
PLEASE COMPLY WITH OUR VEHICLE AND TRAFFIC LAWS.
IT PROTECTS OUR MOHAWK CHILDREN
WE WISH YOU A SAFE AND ENJOYABLE VISIT
"NIAWEN"
(THANK YOU)

ANIMAL WORDS IN MOHAWK

- **A'NÓ:WARA (AH'-NOH-WAH-LAH)**
  TURTLE

- **SKA'NYONHSA (SGA'-NYOONH-SAH)**
  MOOSE

- **SÓ:RA (ZO-LAH)**
  DUCK

- **TSIKARA'TANYA'KS (JEE-GA-LA'-DUN'-YUKS)**
  FROG

- **TSYOKWARIS (JOE-GWA-LEES)**
  RED-WINGED BLACKBIRD

GET THE FACTS!

It's thought that fewer than 1,000 Mohawk speakers are left. However, there's a movement to save this language. It's still taught to Mohawk children who will pass it on to their children. It can be seen on signs in Mohawk territory too.

SOME FAMOUS PLACE NAMES COME FROM THE MOHAWK LANGUAGE. FOR EXAMPLE, CANADA COMES FROM KANÁ:TA, WHICH MEANS "TOWN."

MEETING THE EUROPEANS

The Mohawk were the first people of the confederacy to meet European explorers because they were the farthest east. The French came upon the Mohawk in 1534. The Mohawk met the Dutch in 1609 and the British in 1664. Sadly, many Mohawk died of European illnesses, such as smallpox.

The Mohawk signed a **treaty** with Dutch explorers called the **Covenant** Chain in the early 1600s. Soon other peoples of the Haudenosaunee had agreements as part of the Covenant Chain. The Haudenosaunee traded furs for guns and other European goods.

THE LOOK AND COLORS OF THE BEADS USED IN WAMPUM BELTS HAD MEANINGS. THE BELTS COULD HELP PEOPLE REMEMBER HISTORY AND LAWS.

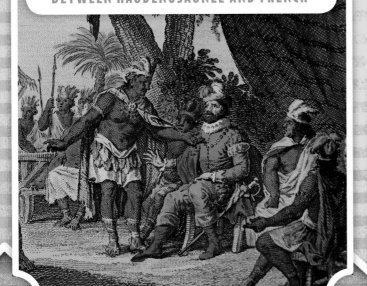

ILLUSTRATION OF 16TH-CENTURY MEETING BETWEEN HAUDENOSAUNEE AND FRENCH

WAMPUM
BEADS MADE FROM WHITE AND PURPLE SHELLS USED FOR CEREMONIES AND DECORATIONS

BROKEN TREATY

The Covenant Chain agreement said the Dutch and Mohawk would live in friendship and peace forever. In 1664, the Dutch gave up New York to the British. The British took their place in the Covenant Chain.

In 1753, a Mohawk leader named Theyanoguin, also called Hendrick, met with British governor George Clinton. Theyanoguin said the British had not been honoring their treaty. They had been cheating Mohawk out of land, among other problems. Theyanoguin believed Mohawk were no longer being treated with respect. He said the Covenant Chain was broken.

THIS IS A COPY OF A COVENANT CHAIN WAMPUM BELT THAT RECORDED THE AGREEMENT BETWEEN THE BRITISH AND HAUDENOSAUNEE.

THEYANOGUIN

THEYANOGUIN
BORN: AROUND 1680
DIED: 1755

GET THE FACTS!

The British recognized that the Covenant Chain was important. They needed to be **allies** with the Mohawk and the other nations of the Haudenosaunee Confederacy for many reasons. In 1754, a ceremony was held to restore the agreement.

AMERICAN WARS

The French and Indian War was fought from 1754 to 1763. France and Great Britain fought over control of North American land. At the start of the war, most Mohawk chose to support their allies, the British. Theyanoguin was killed in action in a battle. France lost much of their American territory at the war's end.

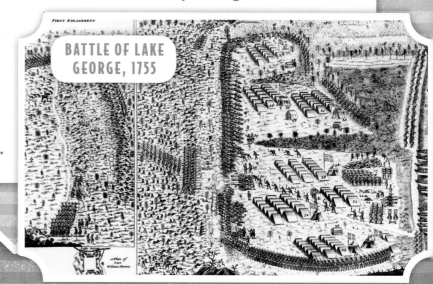

BATTLE OF LAKE GEORGE, 1755

THAYENDANEGEA
BORN: 1743
DIED: 1807

GET THE FACTS!

Some Mohawk chose the side of the French during the French and Indian War. Many lived in French territory in Canada. Others supported the French because they seemed more interested in gaining trading rights than land in North America.

THEYANOGUIN

The American Revolution began in 1775. This war between American colonists and the British divided the Haudenosaunee Confederacy. Mohawk leader Thayendanegea—also called Joseph Brant—supported the British. The British government promised the Mohawk land.

BURNING VILLAGES

The Mohawk people suffered greatly because of their alliance with the British during the American Revolution. General George Washington ordered the destruction of Haudenosaunee settlements. Many Mohawk died when American soldiers attacked them, burned down villages, and destroyed crops.

EVEN HAUDENOSAUNEE WHO SUPPORTED THE AMERICANS DURING THE WAR RECEIVED LITTLE SUPPORT AFTER.

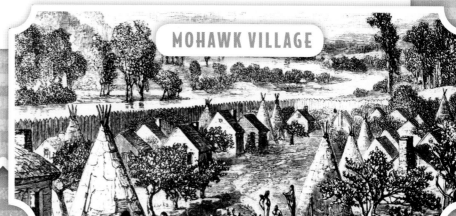

MOHAWK VILLAGE

FORT STANWIX

GET THE FACTS!

The Haudenosaunee people who stayed in the United States signed a treaty at Fort Stanwix in 1784. It set the borders of their territory. They also had to give up western lands they had won from other Native Americans in the late 1600s.

The Treaty of Paris was signed in 1783 to end the war. It set up a border between the United States and Canada through Mohawk territory. Thayendanegea and many other Mohawk fled to Canada, where the British government gave them 1,200 square miles (3,100 sq km) on the Grand River in Ontario.

MOHAWK ON RESERVATIONS

After the war, Mohawk **reservations** were established in Canada and the United States. In fact, one is located in both countries. St. Regis Mohawk Reservation is called Akwesasne Reserve on the Canadian side. Other Mohawk settlements are the Wahta, Kanesatake, Tyendinaga, and Kahnawake territories in Canada.

MOHAWK ATTENDED SCHOOLS THAT ONLY TAUGHT ABOUT WHITE HISTORY.

PRIMER,

FOR THE USE OF THE

MOHAWK CHILDREN,

To acquire the SPELLING and READING of their own, as well as to get acquainted with the ENGLISH, Tongue; which for that Purpose is put on the opposite Page.

WAERIGHWAGHSAWE IKSAONGOENWA

Tſiwaondad-derighhonny Kaghyadoghſera; Nayon-deweyeſtaghk ayeweanaghnodon ayeghyàdow Ka-niyenkehàga Kaweanondaghkouh; Dyorheaſ-hàga oni tſinihadiweanotea.

(❀)

LONDON,

PRINTED BY C. BUCKTON, GREAT PULTNEY-STREET. 1786.

CANADA

KAHNAWAKE
KANESATAKE
WAHTA
AKWESASNE
TYENDINAGA
SIX NATIONS
Lake Huron
Lake Ontario
Lake Erie
MAINE
VT
NH
NY
MA
CT
RI
PA
NJ

Mohawk people were forced to take on the **culture** of white people. They had to wear clothes like those of the whites and practice Christianity. Mohawk children were sent to schools to learn English. They were taught European and American history, but not their own.

FAMOUS FOR FEARLESSNESS

Mohawk people live and work on and off reservations. In the 1880s, some Mohawk were found to have a special skill in construction. During that time, a bridge was being built across the St. Lawrence River onto the Kahnawake Reservation near Montreal, Canada. A railroad company hired Mohawk workers to move supplies.

The company soon discovered Mohawk men could climb the highest beams of the bridge without fear. Since they were unafraid of such great heights, they were hired to help on the bridge. Soon, other job opportunities opened up.

THE MOHAWK'S FEARLESSNESS IN HIGH-RISE CONSTRUCTION IS REMEMBERED AND ADMIRED. MANY STILL WORK AS STEELWORKERS TODAY.

GET THE FACTS!

Some Mohawk moved to New York City to work on tall buildings, or skyscrapers, being built there. The Mohawk have worked on the Empire State Building, the United Nations building, the World Trade Center, Madison Square Garden, and One World Trade Center.

27

MODERN MOHAWK PEOPLE

Mohawk people today live much like other Americans and Canadians. At the same time, they're trying to keep their culture and **traditions** alive. It's believed there are about 47,000 Mohawk descendants today.

GET THE FACTS!

Some Mohawk disagree with the establishment of casinos on their lands. They think it harms their culture. The Kanatsiohareke Mohawk Community in Central New York was established in 1993 to help Mohawk return to their traditional ways.

In modern times, Mohawk are still fighting for their historical lands. They're also fighting businesses that have polluted some of their territory and waterways. In addition, Mohawk disagree about whether reservations should have **casinos** as a means of making money. Reservation governments deal with many issues and continue to work to make sure the Mohawk people are respected.

GLOSSARY

ally One of two or more people or groups who work together.

breechcloth A cloth that covers the hips.

casino A place where people play games of chance to try and win money.

ceremony An event to honor or celebrate something.

confederacy A group of people or states joined in a common purpose.

constitution The basic laws by which a country or state is governed.

covenant A formal agreement.

culture The beliefs and ways of life of a group of people.

decorate To add something to make a piece of clothing look special.

descended Coming after another in a family.

natural resource A usable supply of something found in nature.

reservation Land set aside by the government for Native Americans.

tradition A long-practiced custom.

treaty An agreement between countries or peoples.

FOR MORE INFORMATION

BOOKS

Corneau, Michelle. *Strong Stories: Kanyen'kehà:ka Stories.* Nanaimo, BC: Strong Nations Publishing, 2016.

Lajiness, Katie. *Mohawk.* Minneapolis, MN: Big Buddy Books, 2019.

Nixon, Dolores. *Mohawk Nation.* Collingwood, ON: Beech Street Books, 2018.

WEBSITES

Mohawk Indian Fact Sheet
bigorrin.org/mohawk_kids.htm
Learn about Mohawk arts, crafts, and music.

Mohawk Nation Council of Chiefs
www.mohawknation.org/
Read about this Mohawk government and its history.

INDEX